C000057917

I LOVE WRESTLING MASKS

COLORING BOOK

SPEEDY
PUBLISHING

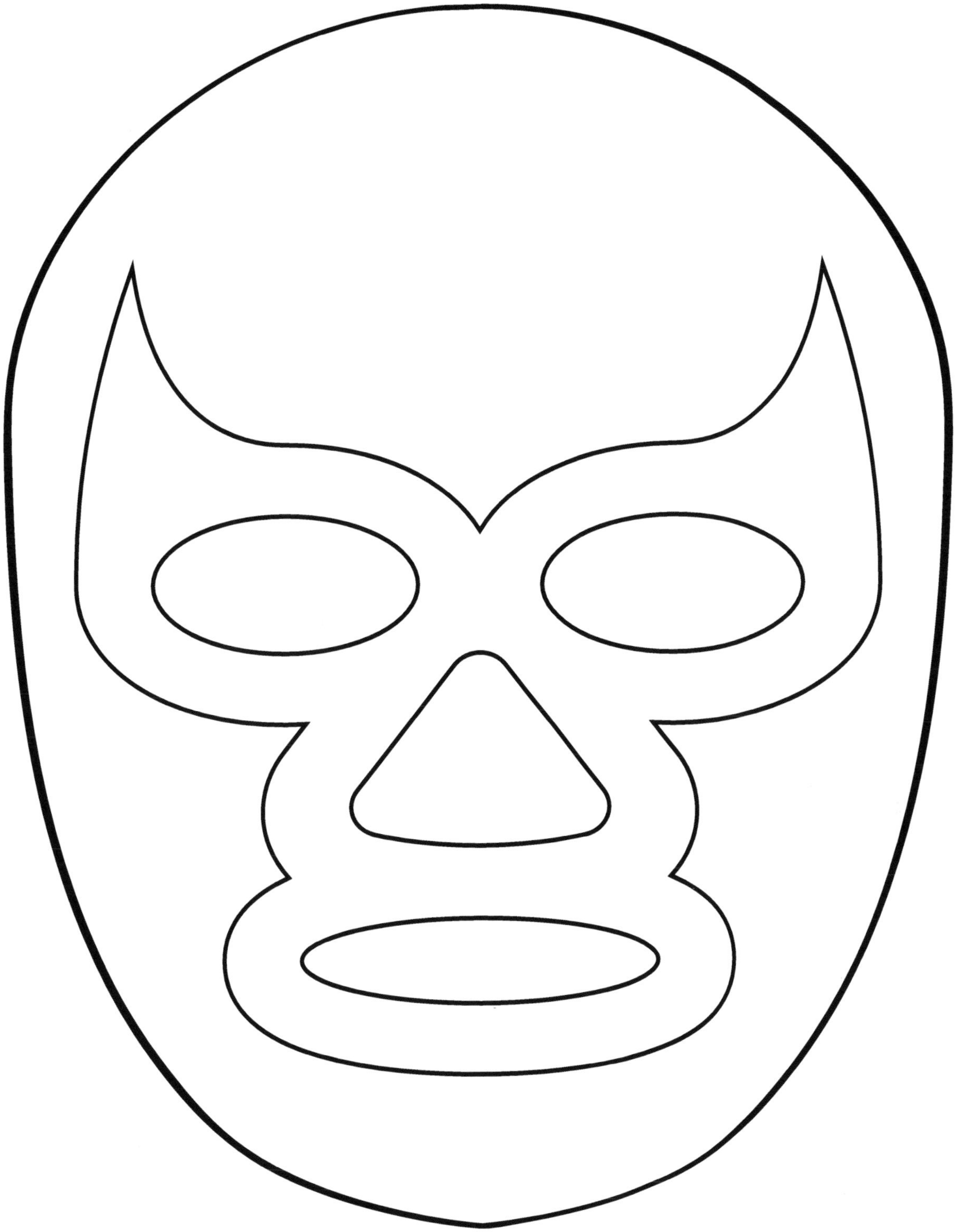

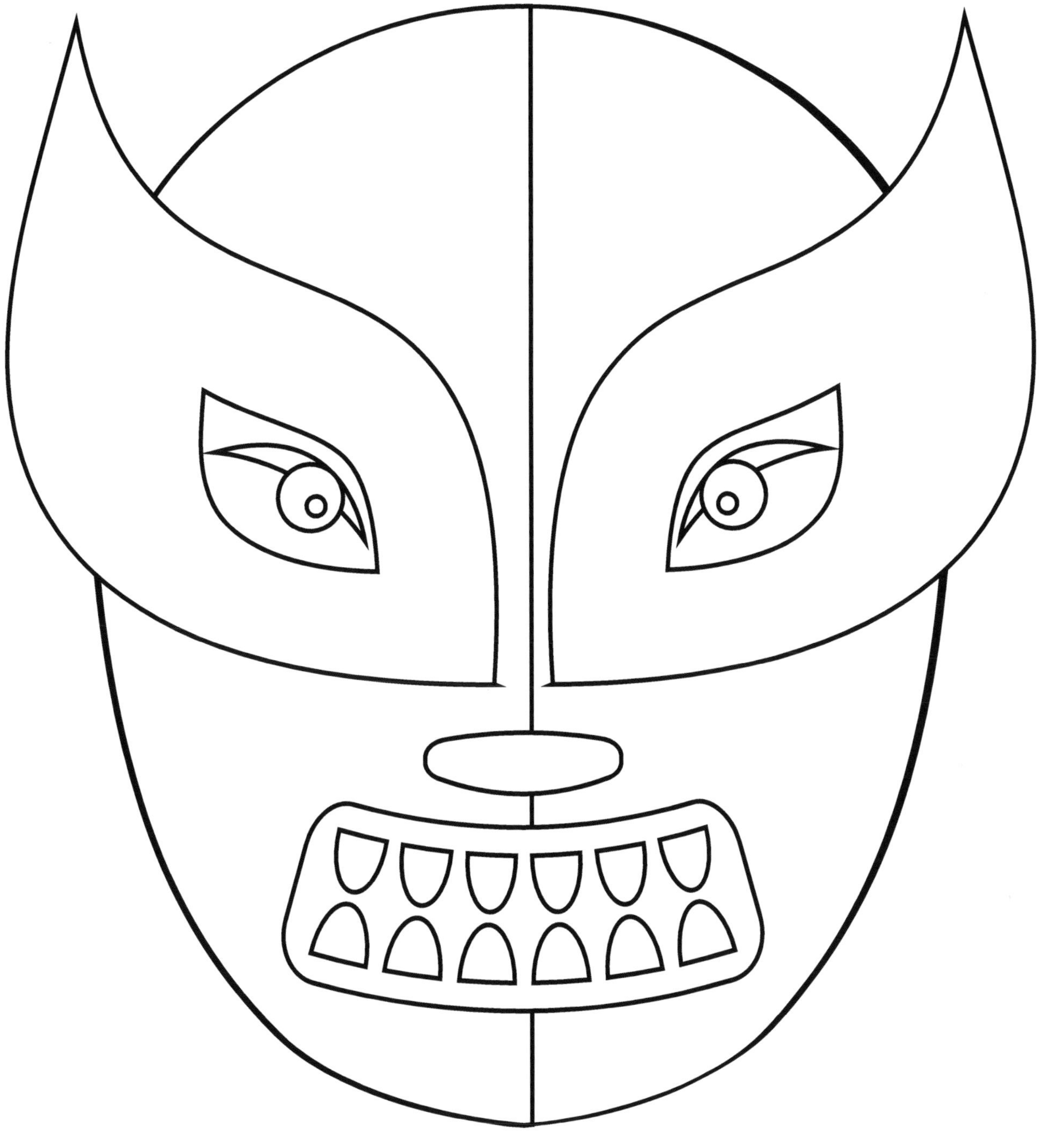

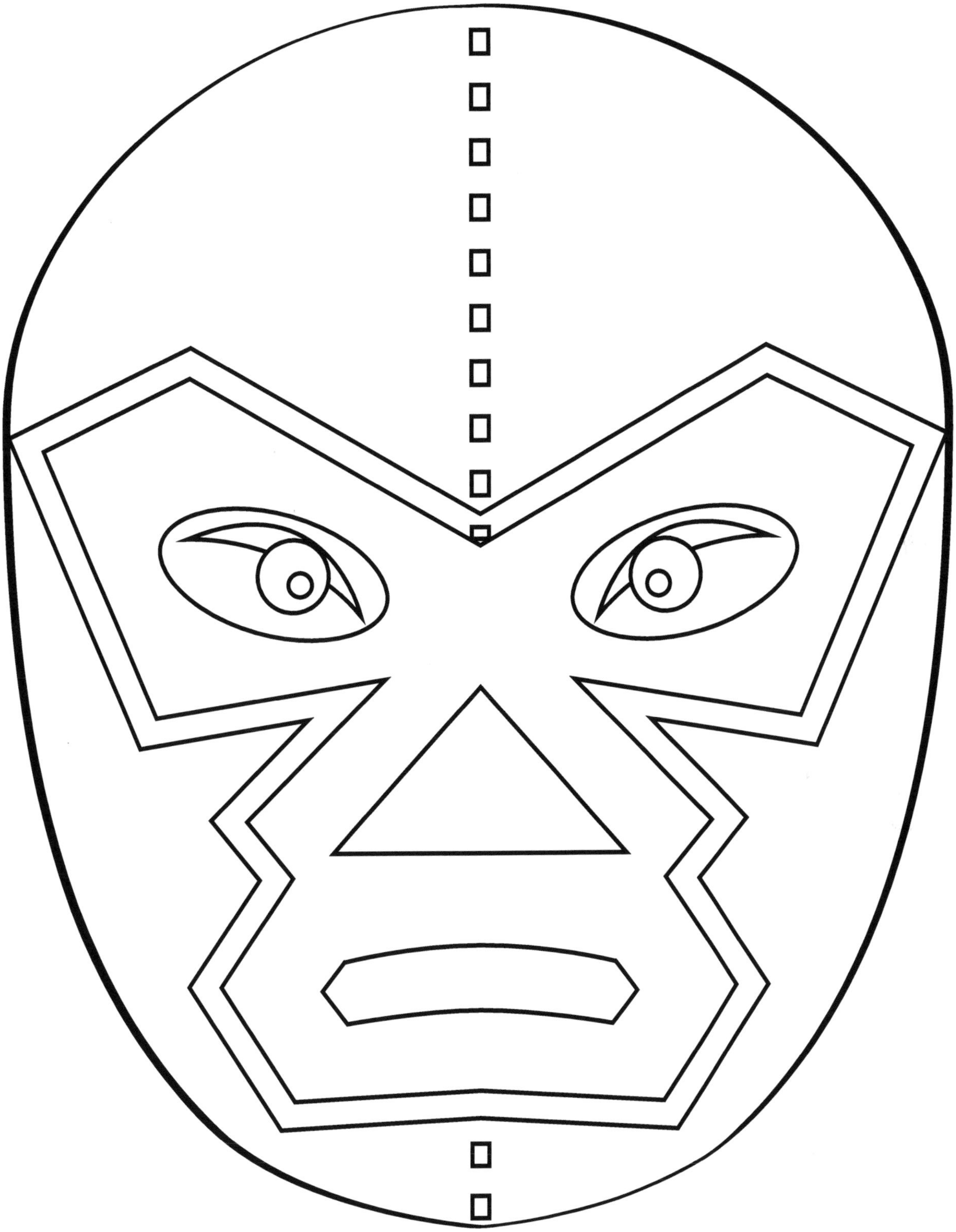

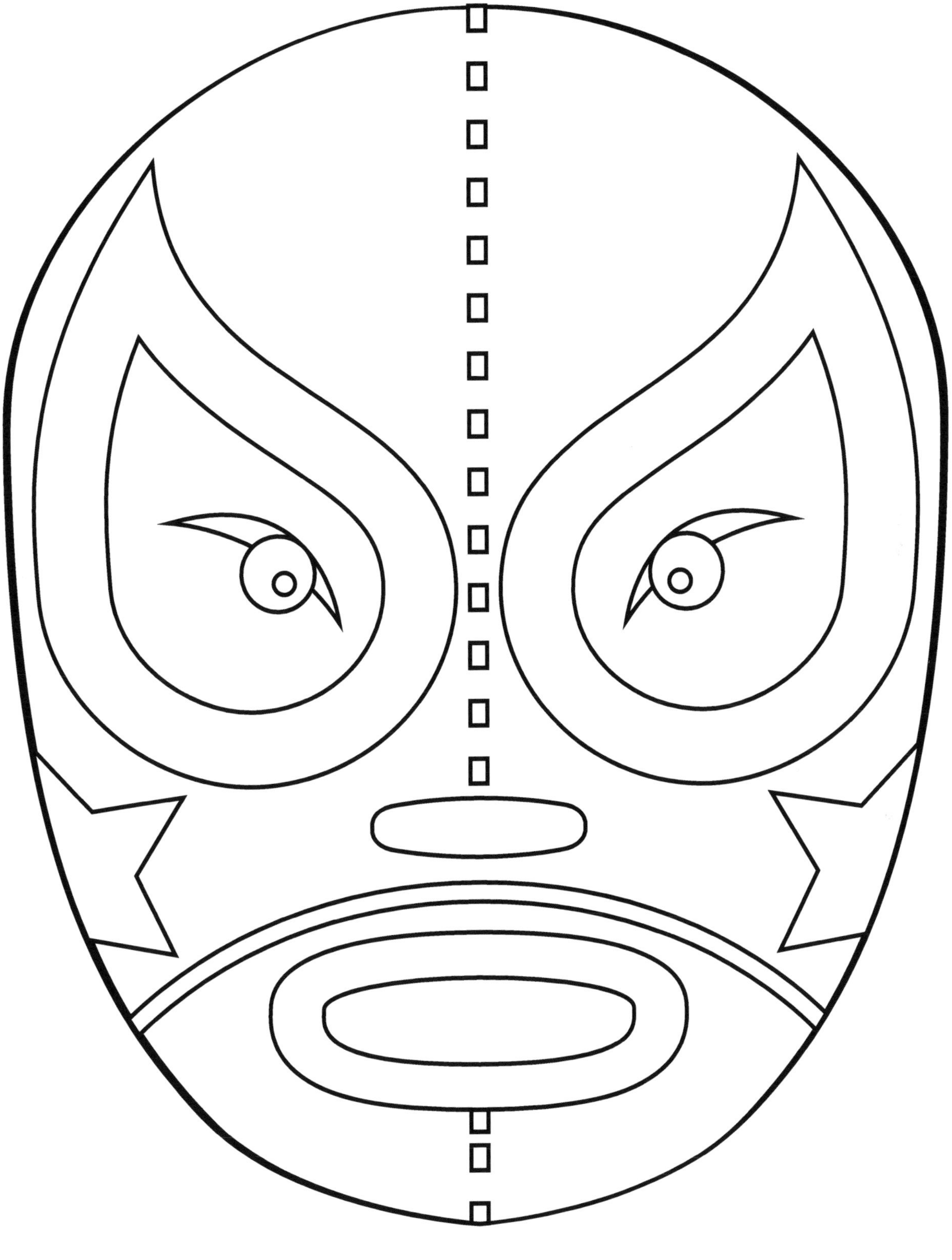

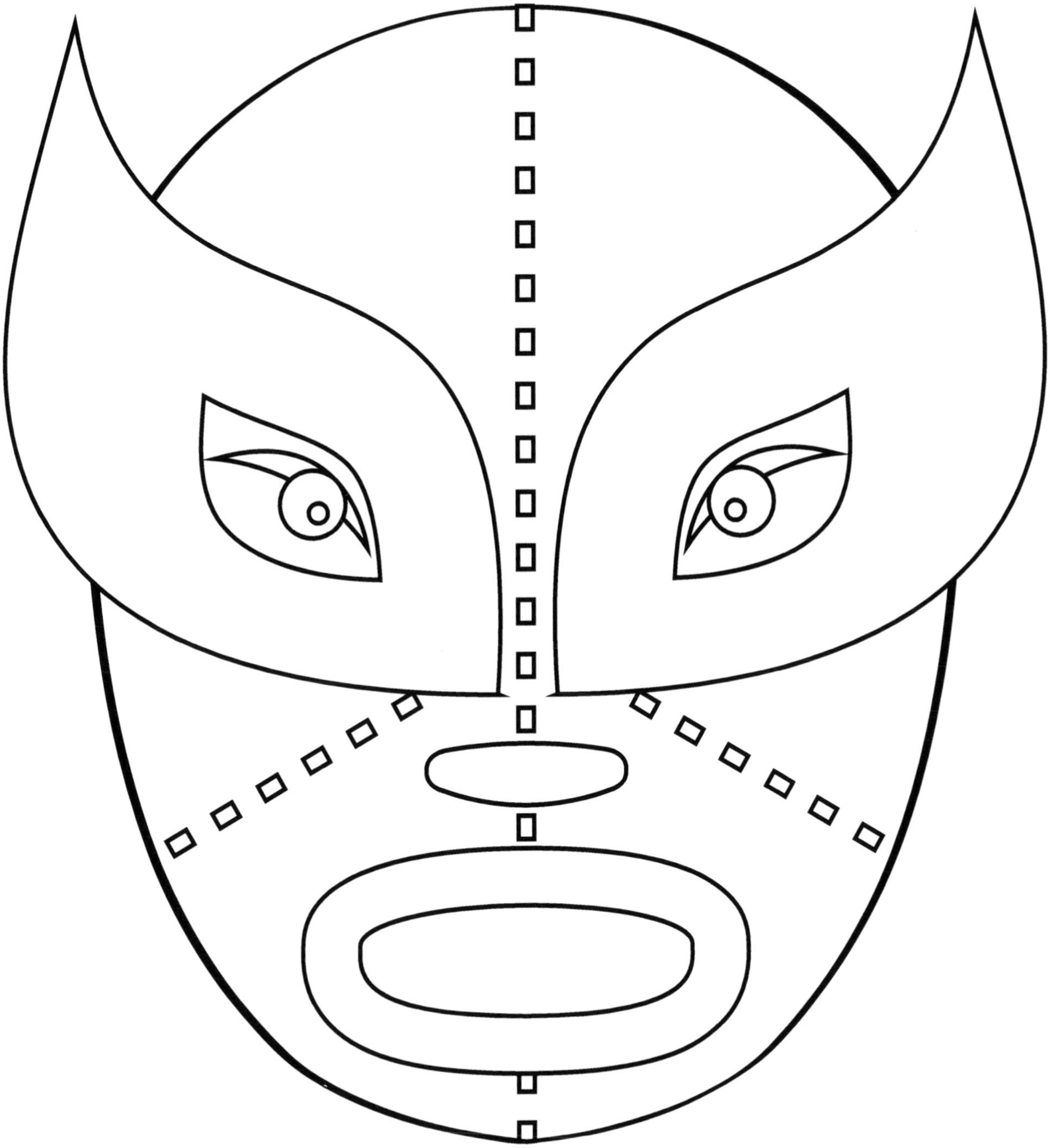

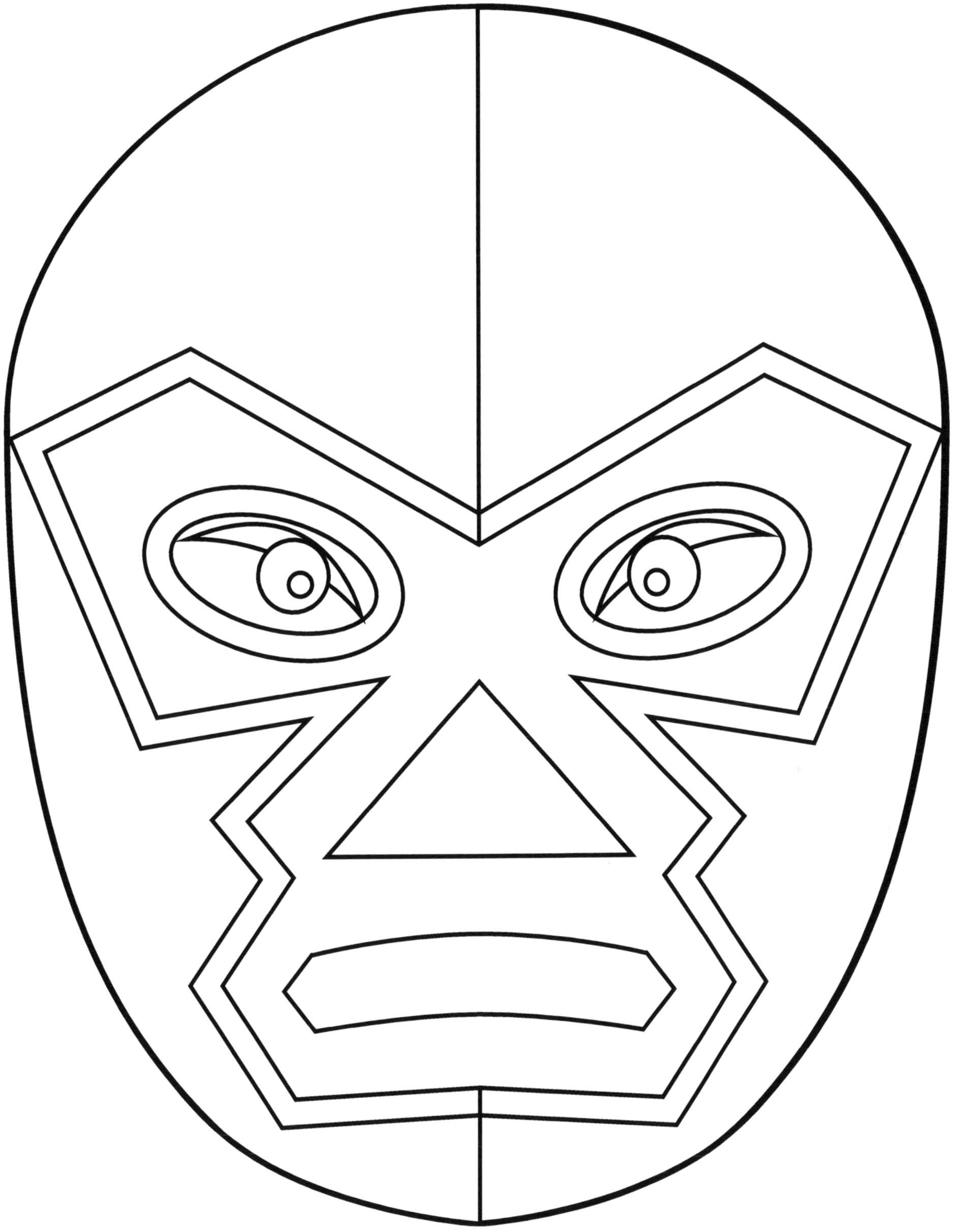